Reposed

poems by

Charlotte McCaffrey

Finishing Line Press
Georgetown, Kentucky

Reposed

For the boys

Copyright © 2017 by Charlotte McCaffrey
ISBN 978-1-63534-135-5 First Edition
All rights reserved under International and Pan-American Copyright Conventions.
No part of this book may be reproduced in any manner whatsoever without written permission from the publisher, except in the case of brief quotations embodied in critical articles and reviews.

ACKNOWLEDGMENTS

Grateful acknowledgement is made to the following publications where previous versions of these poems first appeared:

Confluence : "Adam Workman" (originally titled "Portraits of the Author's Grandmother, Lillian Schermer")

Madison Review: "David" section of "News of Our Summer Siblings" (originally titled "Revival")

Sincere thanks for the support, patience, and feedback through many readings from the Buddha Pumpkin Writing Collective, the Green Heart Writing Collective, and, of course, from Phyllis.

Publisher: Leah Maines

Editor: Christen Kincaid

Cover Art: Jill Friedman

Author Photo: Jill Friedman

Cover Design: Elizabeth Maines

Printed in the USA on acid-free paper.
Order online: www.finishinglinepress.com
        also available on amazon.com

Author inquiries and mail orders:
Finishing Line Press
P. O. Box 1626
Georgetown, Kentucky 40324
U. S. A.

Table of Contents

Testimony 1

Standstill 3

False Pride 4

Pilgrim's Wardrobe 6

Adam Workman 7

Don't Fence Me In 9

Boo 10

Missing Donkeys 11

Weather Report 13

Under the Influence 14

Combat 15

Sybil 17

News of Our Summer Siblings 19

Officer of the Watch 22

Stationed 23

No More Pets 25

Twos and Threes 27

Cannonball 29

Isn't That Something 30

Communion 32

Settlement 34

TESTIMONY

When my father decided to sell his house—
just him now, too much room—
he called Mr. Bonds, who did estate sales
and was told everything
would be taken care of.

Do you want us to come help you?
we children asked him from six states away.
No, no, he said. *Mr. Bonds will be here.
Movers will pack and move me. It's just
a few blocks away.*

He was our father, a lawyer
a life-long military man.
If he said no, we didn't question it.
We told him what to save.
He said he made a list.

But there was no list.
Moving was too much for him.
We should have known.

My father let Mr. Bonds
sell almost everything
including the family photo albums—
hundreds of pictures
from our childhood
ordered and labeled by my father
years ago, when he was old
but not this old.

Some stranger, some collector
of other people's lives
had them now.

A few images are here
retrieved, developed
transferred back to paper
black and white
saved.

STANDSTILL

I stand next to my father
barely come up to his waist
sunhat pulled so far down
that my eyes are lost
in shadow
mouth rigid
arms stick-like
hands clench at my sides.

He stands hatless
arms akimbo
broad smile on his face
eyes squint from the sun.
He chuckles at my fury
the details of which—
on this particular day—
I don't recall.

Later, our relative
positions change.
I care for him at the end.

But we repeat these
early standoffs
many times:
my rage at not being
seen or heard
his bemusement

as if he were holding me
at arm's length, palm pressed
against my forehead
laughing while I
swing and swing and swing.

FALSE PRIDE

My mother stands next to
our black '51 Buick
one small son on either side
infant daughter—me—in her arms
her broad straw hat at a slant
best church clothes on all of us.
My father takes this picture.
My mother doesn't smile.

She always hated her teeth
hid them whenever
a camera came near.
What she wanted was braces.
Never to hear
"Bucky Beaver" again.

Her mouth gave her trouble
most of her life.
*Morning and night no one
there to make us brush,* she said.
*We'd get coins from Mama's purse
while she slept and buy cookies
for breakfast on the way to school.
Only went to a dentist
to get one pulled.*
Once grown, she suffered through
crowns, bridges, root canals.

In her later years, she had
teeth she loved, took them out
each night and carefully put
them away like jewelry.
She smiled more often
laughed at the camera.

But on this Sunday morning
she poses stiffly
lips tightly sealed
over her flaw.

PILGRIM'S WARDROBE

My brothers and I sit in train cars
sized for elves
or teacups meant for giants
mouse-eared pilgrims
in this cartoon land
where fantasy
is the rule. When we leave
we take our ears with us.

At home, one of my brothers
gave his to me.
They're stupid and for babies
he snickered. Soon after
he gave me his teddy bear
saying the same thing.
My mother asked him
Are you sure?

I loved those hand-me-downs
but had my heart set on others:
his yellow dump trucks
silver six-shooter
his clothes.

I began asking for his
outgrown t-shirts and jeans.
My reluctant mother allowed
it, watching me wordlessly
as I dressed. I wore them
almost every day
in the summer.

Once my breasts
began to sprout
she insisted
on bras and blouses, ripped
up the t-shirts for rags.

ADAM WORKMAN

A Royal typewriter is fixed in front
of my snow-headed grandmother, Lillian.
She is berthed behind a broad oak desk
the length of my bed, in the office
of the Gulf Coast News Digest—
the union newspaper she edits.

The desk, a chair, the floor
hold old editions, teetering
stacks of paper, ashtrays.
Photographs of southern politicians
priests and longshoremen hang
cheek to jowl on the walls.

Lillian looks up at us children
through thick, black-framed glasses.
We peer from behind our mother
who snapped the photo.
We are early for our midday visit
but today Lillian is smiling.

For many years, she wrote a column
called "Adam Workman"
relating news of weddings
baby arrivals, illness, death—
milestones in the lives of the men
who worked the Mobile docks.

Sometimes Lillian reflected
on national events. When she
came out against the Vietnam War
she established her credentials
by citing a grandfather
who lost his leg fighting
for the Confederacy.

This assured that she wasn't vilified
by the conservative union members—
a kind of logic that worked
in that time and place.

DON'T FENCE ME IN

The pistol hangs by his side
holstered. He stands alone
against the back wall
of a small brick house.

A glint flashes
off the gun. He squints
against the sun in his eyes—
never a good situation
in a face-off—even this one
with the camera
our mother has trained
on my five-year-old brother
and his Roy Rogers six-shooter.

He's not saddled
with me, his little sister
or roped together
with our older brother.
Not lost in a herd-shot
of cousins. He holds
both arms out from his sides
as if to say—

Look! Some room for me!

Once grown, Brian chose
the practice of law—
a field well-suited
to showdowns
and freeing people
from tight squeezes.

BOO

Lips pouty
raven hair swept up
my great-aunt Ruby gazes
into the camera.
Papa had to beat the boys off with a stick,
her sister, Lillian, allowed.
But Papa missed one.

Unmarried, pregnant
Alabama 1922
Ruby went to the country doctor
who would later become
her father-in-law
who would also sign
her mother's death certificate:
Carcinoma of the uterus
written in his beautiful
steady longhand.

Dr. Cawthorn ended her pregnancy
losing his own grandchild
and, by some slip, any others
who might have followed.

Ruby—we called her Boo—favored
cheap grocery store wine
reds of course
and kept beagles
obese house dogs
that trailed behind her
their bellies grazing the floor
as they waited for their treats.

She doted on Dr. Cawthorn's son
and the two husbands who followed.
Dogs and bottle always at hand
she outlived them all.

MISSING DONKEYS

Crepe paper and balloons hang
from the walls of our dining room
in southern California.
My friends and I wear shiny
cone-shaped hats
for my fifth birthday party.
We blow party favors that honk
and uncurl like decorated
frog tongues.

My father spins us one by one
until we lurch, blindfolded
try to Pin the Tail on the Donkey.
When the game ends
my mother serves us
the chocolate cake she has baked.

Two of my friends lived next door
a boy and a girl, twins
from Mexico. They had a birthday
party too and their father
raised and lowered
a donkey piñata covered
with rainbow-striped crepe paper.
Blindfolded, I swung wildly
and missed.
Later we had soft flour
tortillas their mother made.

Soon after the parties
a for-sale sign appeared
in front of their house.
Once they were gone
two new friends appeared—
an imaginary boy and girl.
A few months later
when my father got orders
and we moved to Boston
I took them with me.

WEATHER REPORT

I am planted waist-deep
in a drift, bundled
in a dark snowsuit
hood pulled up, six years old.
This time last year—Long Beach
eating warm tortillas.
Behind me now
a gabled grey house
on a New England street.

My father's orders
brought us here—duty on the
Coast Guard Cutter McCullough
that sailed out of Boston
monitored weather stations
performed search and rescue
in the North Atlantic.
A pattern of twelve weeks
at sea then home.

Our house breathed differently
when he was gone—
my mother double checking
the doors at night
my brothers and I raucous
our steps and voices loud
as we stomped through the rooms.

I'd never seen snow before.
In the photo, my mouth is open
to catch flakes on my tongue
two front teeth missing
mittened hands raised
as if in wonder
in surrender
to this new weather.

UNDER THE INFLUENCE

My grandfather clutches a large crab
in each hand. Their bright orange
just-boiled color
doesn't show in this faded photo.

Click-click he whispers
moving closer.
Then louder—*Here we come!*
He chases me around the kitchen
pretends to snap the pinchers.
The claws don't scare me
as much as he does.

My grandfather was a good cook
a crack shot, a drunk. He made gumbo
won medals training sharpshooters
while his hands were still steady.
Brewed 'shine in the Alabama hills
during Prohibition.

My grandmother left him
when he wouldn't sober up.
My mother could never
forgive his drinking.

This brief summer vacation
on the Gulf Coast
is the only time I see him
though his love
of alcohol lives
in me, in the family
taking three of the boys so early
casualties of our own war.

COMBAT

A dozen Christmas scenes
light five different living rooms.
Early, black and white photos
show stunted, tinsel-draped trees
strung with big-bulbed lights
a modest pile
of presents underneath.

In later years
the trees—now in color—almost
reach the ceiling, gifts spill
out into the room under strands
of small, twinkly lights.

Ornaments, sold with the photos
dangle from the branches:
tin drums, tiny french horns
ceramic Santas, my mother's angels—
glass, straw, porcelain—
from around the world.

My brothers and I rip the paper
off presents, then hold them up
to the camera: a toy, a book
a disappointing sweater;
in good times, a sled or a bike.

One year, every box
I opened held something pink
or a doll that wet itself.
Long past Santa, I cried
for days, begged my parents
to return them. Worn down
my father took me to Sears.
Get her what she wants, my mother
told him, shaking her head.

I came home with a black, plastic
Tommy gun that looked like the ones
I saw every Thursday night on "Combat."

No one took a picture of that.

SYBIL

The wild card of the family
was Auntie Sybil
my mother's only sibling.

She married an alcoholic
cookie salesman
a rakishly handsome man
of mostly French ancestry
with the last name of Venus.
My cousins and I bolted
out the door to meet him
whenever he weaved
into the driveway, the back seat
of his car full of samples:
Pecan Sandies, Vienna Fingers.

The straw was broken when
he drunkenly shoved my aunt.
Though it left her with four children
to raise on her own, she sent him
packing. We mourned the loss
of all those free cookies.

She is pregnant with her first child
my cousin Cindy, in this photo
taken early in her marriage.
She stands in a doorway, smiling broadly
wears a white blouse and a dark skirt
that balloons around her.
Sybil went on to have
three more children—all boys.

The oldest was named for his father—
Henry Thornton.
We called him Thorne.
Michael, the youngest, died at
twenty-four, strangled by alcohol.

Sybil threatened
to call her middle son Delfen
the brand name of the spermicide
she was using at the time.
I never saw that one coming, she said.
Later, she settled on David.

NEWS OF OUR SUMMER SIBLINGS

My four cousins sprawl
in swim suits
on bleached out
beach towels.

Some summers
we pile in with them.
Our meshed families
packed into a rented cottage
at Gulf Shores
three women seven kids
the dads stay at work.

We wake to the waves
sleep sunburnt on sand-gritty sheets.
Shells collected in waxy Dixie cups
then lined up on window sills.
Rain meant cards on a screened-in porch
always someone to play with.
We squabble conspire tease tattle.

Cindy

Notorious
in her twenties—
booked, fingerprinted, front page
of the Mobile Press Register
charged with harboring
a pig within city limits.
Homer, who lived next door
something of a slob himself
turned her in, complaining
of an odor that Cindy insisted
wasn't there. *Pigs are smart and clean*
she said, *unlike some in this neighborhood.*

Her pig had his own little blanket-lined
pig-house in the back yard.
Cindy later staged a fundraiser at the mall
for the PDF (Porcine Defense Fund), sold
tee shirts that said "Save Grunt", the name of her
pot-bellied cohort. The judge ruled
in their favor, allowing Grunt
to live out his years in sty-lish comfort.

Thorne

My cousin Thorne made the paper as well
a prime spot in the feature section.
He built a three-story tree house
with scrap wood that looked like something
out of Dogpatch but was an impressive feat
for a ten year old—got a quarter page photo.
Hot tempered, always moving
Thorne pitched his cards, cursed us all
when he lost at Canasta.
Once he dug a hole in the backyard
so deep he couldn't get out.
Later told his mother
he just wanted to get away.
Someone finally threw a rope
held on while he pulled himself up.
Fit to be tied she said.

David

David almost made the news
the summer we nearly lost him.
He doesn't remember
just four at the time. The lagoon

seemed safe, his brother, cousins near.
Water only two feet or so
except for the hole a bit off shore
darker, deep where they had dredged
some time ago, never filled in.
We were older, grew bored with him
left, though we knew better and would
regret it, because he kept wading
found the hole and fell in
then just floated, cousins gone, brother gone
until Sybil, in the cottage making lunch
saw him from the window
screamed, raced across the beach
feet almost flying above the sand
and then through the water
until she could scoop him up in her arms
and pound the lagoon out of his lungs
pound his back until someone pulled her off
saying *There, there* and we watched him
sputter back to life, listened to him breathe.

Michael

We did lose Michael.
A kind of drowning.
Another summer
age twenty-four
alcohol choked
the breath out of him.
It took only three lines
in the paper
to recount
his short life.

OFFICER OF THE WATCH

Sporting a beard
wearing his khakis
my father smiles, back
from three months
of sea duty, a young officer
on a Coast Guard ship
patrolling the North Atlantic.

He pulls at his scraggly chin.
Although he lost the contest
to see who could grow
the longest whiskers while at sea
he stands straight
faces the camera.

Years later, he told us
of an incident from one
of those deployments.
As a storm came up—
wind, rain, waves
bowing their heads
rocking the vessel
he sent the sailors out
to secure the deck.

I sent twenty and got nineteen back.
I left them out there too long
or maybe that one fellow didn't
come in when he should have.
Don't know which. His voice cracked.
We just couldn't get to him.

Did you have to tell the family?
I asked.
No, he murmured.
There was a chaplain for that.

STATIONED

My mother, caught off guard
smiles broadly, revealing
those unfortunate teeth.
She stands at the sink
in the kitchen of a house
she did not see until the day
we moved in. She sings softly
while she washes dishes
hymns and old songs—
Shall We Gather at the River
You Made Me Love You

Each time the military gave him
orders, my father traveled ahead
found a place, left her
to direct the movers, mobilize
and pack up the kids.
He went with her wishes
for a kitchen window
a tree in the yard
sometimes finding one
but rarely both.

Most nights she hurried
to cook supper
finally wresting herself
from novels and soaps
that eased her through drab days
while the rest of us
engaged with the world.

Water snarled on the stove
while she scrubbed potatoes
and flayed carrots
cleaning off what she called
the afterdirt.

While the meatloaf or casserole cooked
she'd call us in to start homework
before our father got home.
Then she tidied up
tending to the little territory
she occupied.
Not chosen, but hers.

NO MORE PETS

Our fat brawler Sam
orange tabby tomcat
peers up at the camera
from inside an empty
washing machine
where he has been napping.
He often comes home
with roughed-up ears
missing patches of fur.

On a Saturday afternoon
after we'd received orders to move
six thousand miles away
my father took him to the pound.

This was the second time
we'd left an animal behind.
The first was a beagle-ish mutt
named Sheba. After Sam
my mother said
No more pets.

But on a river in rural Alabama
my father, then retired
found an abandoned kitten
named her Miz Kate.

He caught sunfish for her.
She'd slap her paw on them, watch
them flop on the dock awhile
before carrying them off.
She brought him dead snakes, field mice.
They'd nap together on the back porch.
He kept her in at night.

Dogs, also left behind
ran wild in a pack.
When Kate didn't come home
one evening my father searched
the woods, found tufts
of her fur at the base of a pine.

Sometime later, he discovered a box
of puppies left by the river bank.
No pound, he said.
Kinder than drowning.
Took his .22
shot all five of them.

TWOS AND THREES

My older brothers
often appear
as a crew-cut twosome.

Here they crouch
over red plastic bricks
or green army men
shooing me away
from their cities and wars.

My mother snaps them
as they lace up roller skates
pull sleds up Pearl Street hill
ride off together on black
three-speed Schwinns.

They grin in swim trunks
frown in blue and white
school uniforms.
Almost angelic, they pose
in black and white cassocks
altar boys lighting candles
three years apart.

Sunday morning
after mass, they rolled
on the living room floor.
Dad in his undershirt
wrestled with his boys
the three of them dissolved
in laughter.

I had to call my father
many years later
tell him that his older son
was dead. Phil hid the worst
of his drinking so I knew
Dad believed me
when I said *Pneumonia*.

CANNONBALL

Sister Catherine Agnes
a portly nun in a black habit
was feared
by the entire second grade.
Behind her back
we called her *Cannonball*.

In the photo she stands outside
the church next to me
her arm clenched
tightly around my shoulders.
My head tilts at a strange angle
a forced and slightly panicked
smile on my face.

Sister seeded us with her stories:

Students immolated in a school fire
skeletons found still
seated at their desks.
At eight, we never asked why
they didn't run
why the desks weren't burnt too.

Children rushed to the hospital
fingernails bitten and swallowed
lodged in their stomachs.

Sister reminded us to pray
and to kiss our mothers goodbye
each morning because Jesus
might call them at any time.

We bowed our heads
knuckled our little hands
together into clammy
clenched balls.

ISN'T THAT SOMETHING

More photos of him
than any of us— my brother Phil
first child, first grandchild
first boy in a generation.
Someone with a camera
always finding him.
Photos mailed to all the relatives.

This allowed us to salvage
enough childhood pictures to fill a board
at his funeral service.

Alcohol—social lubricant
for my awkward brother—
made his life easier until
it didn't. By then
he couldn't put it down.

Phil had few friends
growing up. He rode
his bike, liked to swim
but loved his books
stamp collection
science experiments
that stunk up the house.

He asked a boy over to play
one Saturday afternoon.
My mother warned
my brother Brian and me—
our mouths agape at this news—
to steer clear.

In the vacant lot next door
Phil and the boy tossed a ball
back and forth. Bunched
around a small window
the three of us watched.

Brian gasped, *He's playing catch!*
With a friend! I whispered.
Yes, my mother smiled.
Isn't that something?

COMMUNION

Stiff white dress and veil
head bowed, hands steepled
I piously ignore my father
and his camera as I walk down
the center aisle of our church
about to receive
my first communion.

Monsignor Fisher
an elderly priest in our parish
places the wafer on my tongue.
Don't chew it! the nuns had dictated.
Afraid to move a muscle
of my face, I let it melt.

Before we knew anything
of the clergy-crimes
my entire family left the Church.

Maybe the edicts against
divorce
being gay
birth control
pushed even
my Irish-Catholic raised father
my mother, the convert
out the vestibule door.

Better to leave than believe
all three of their children
were condemned.

Never a gambler
my father returned
in his final years.

My mother never went back.
She abandoned the trappings as well—
her missal and rosary.

But at night, bedroom door left open
I heard her whisper
her homemade prayers.

SETTLEMENT

The photographs
that hang in my house
are of strangers
culled from antique shows
flea markets, estate sales—
pictures that sat
piled in boxes
or waiting in albums
next to signs that read:
Find a Family.

Such a simple
if incomplete
remedy.

My walls now hold
crew-cut boys with bicycles
a polka dot-aproned mother
a balding father who grins
as a little girl in a blue dress
grasps his hand.

My glance rests easy
on these smiling stand-ins.
A war is over.
The nineteen-fifties
stretch brightly ahead.

Perhaps in a room
in another house
someone sits
wonders
and looks curiously
at my mother
my father
my brothers
me.

Charlotte McCaffrey was born in Mobile, Alabama. During her childhood, her family moved around the country, from California and Massachusetts to Maryland and Hawaii. She graduated from Washington University in St. Louis and then spent many years in the Midwest working as a chef. In 1989, she moved to northern California where she was an elementary special education teacher for 25 years.

Her work has appeared in *Borderlands, Bayou, The Comstock Review, Hampden-Sydney Poetry Review, Poetry International, Poet Lore, Sojourner, Women's Studies Quarterly*, and many other journals and anthologies. Currently, she is retired and lives with her partner in the San Francisco Bay area where she writes, gardens, cooks, and dotes on her dogs.

www.ingramcontent.com/pod-product-compliance
Lightning Source LLC
LaVergne TN
LVHW041603070426
835507LV00011B/1278